Living with
Change

By Loma R. Meyer

Edited by Thomas J. Doyle

Editorial assistant: Phoebe Wellman

Contents

Change— Threat or Opportunity?

Focusing Our Sights

In this session we will look at the struggle people experience as they face change. We will recognize change as an inevitable part of the human experience. Then we will explore the changes caused by the fall of people into sin and how these changes impact our lives and the lives of those around us. We will discover how change threatens people as well as provides them opportunities. We will identify ways in which God has blessed us through change and will thank God for changing us through the Gospel. Finally, we will look at changes we desire God to work in us so that we can better face uncertainties caused by change.

Focusing Our Attention

1. Write your definition of the word *change*. Compare your definition with those of others in the group. Try to reach consensus for a definition of *change*.

2. Share an incident of change from your life. Use the following questions to guide your sharing.

a. Was the change inevitable? Why or why not?

b. How was the change an opportunity, a threat, or both?

c. How did you feel as you anticipated and then experienced the change?

d. How did others feel as they anticipated and then experienced the change?

Focusing on the Issue

As we journey through life, we are confronted with many changes. People react to change differently. Social attitudes, religious beliefs, and culture all affect our attitude and response to change. People usually respond to change at one of three basic levels. They may

- keep things going as is, except tinker with a few things to make "it" work better;
- make changes that, for the most part, are in agreement with the wishes and opinions of others; or
- make changes that seem for the better, even though others may have strong feelings against the proposed changes. The changes may involve scrapping the present "system" and introducing a completely new "system."

Think about the differences between the three levels of change.

1. At what level do you generally respond to change at work? in the home? in the church? in the community? in the nation?

2. What accounts for the differences in how you respond to change in the home? church? community? nation?

3. Check all the things that apply to you as you anticipate change in your life.

___ I feel as though I am no longer needed in this situation.

___ I have to do a lot more work in order to accomplish the change.

___ I will have greater opportunity to relate to others.

___ I will become angry.

___ I worry about the impact of the change.

___ I become impatient with those around me because they do/don't embrace the change.

___ I am accused of not "being with it" because I question or am against the change.

___ I will lose friends if I speak for or against the change.

___ I will become alienated from my family if I speak for or against the change.

___ I examine my attitude and feelings about the change.

___ I have greater stress in my life.

___ I worry that the uncertainty that comes with change is not worth the progress it may provide.

___ I fear the change will not work.

___ I worry whether or not the change is God's will.

___ Other _______________________________________

____

____

Go back over the list. Put an *O* next to the statement(s) that, in your opinion, present an opportunity. Put a *T* next to the statement(s) that, in your opinion, pose a threat. In some instances you may want to put both a *T* and an *O* in front of a statement(s).

4. Identify three "good" changes that occurred in your life during the past decade.

5. When you initially anticipated or experienced each of the changes, was it a threat or an opportunity? How did the change turn out to be "good?"

Focusing on God's Word

Our first parents, Adam and Eve, once lived completely holy and happy lives in the Garden of Eden. Then things changed. Read **Genesis 3:1–7** to review how this change came about.

9

Now the serpent was more crafty than any of the wild animals the LORD God had made. He said to the woman, "Did God really say, 'You must not eat from any tree in the garden'?" The woman said to the serpent, "We may eat fruit from the trees in the garden, but God did say, 'You must not eat fruit from the tree that is in the middle of the garden, and you must not touch it, or you will die.'"

"You will not surely die," the serpent said to the woman. "For God knows that when you eat of it your eyes will be opened, and you will be like God, knowing good and evil."

When the woman saw that the fruit of the tree was good for food and pleasing to the eye, and also desirable for gaining wisdom, she took some and ate it. She also gave some to her husband, who was with her, and he ate it. Then the eyes of both of them were opened, and they realized they were naked; so they sewed fig leaves together and made coverings for themselves.

1. What change did Adam and Eve experience? (See also **Genesis 3:8–24.**)

2. How did this change affect their lives?

3. How has this change affected our lives?

In spite of the choice made by Adam and Eve, God provided a plan to change us back into what He intended us to be.

For He chose us in Him before the creation of the world to be holy and blameless in His sight. In love He predestined us to be adopted as His sons through Jesus Christ, in accordance with His pleasure and will—to the praise of His glorious grace, which He has freely given us in the One He loves. In Him we have redemption through His blood, the forgiveness of sins, in accordance with the riches of God's grace that He lavished on us with all wisdom and understanding. And He made known to us the mystery of His will according to His good pleasure, which He purposed in Christ. (**Ephesians 1:4–9**)

4. Underline the change God brought about for us when because of sin we were separated from Him.

5. Draw a cross next to the means through which God would bring about this change.

6. With the change God provided to us through Jesus Christ, He gave wisdom and understanding. He also made known to us "the

11

mystery of His will." How can these gifts assist us as we face change?

Focusing on My Life

God promises to continue to provide us with wisdom and understanding through His Word as we anticipate and experience change. God's love for us revealed in the person and work of His Son Jesus enables us to confess, "Yet not as I will, but as You will" (**Matthew 26:39**), in the face of change. Read the following Bible passages, which have brought comfort to many especially during times of change in their lives.

Are not two sparrows sold for a penny? Yet not one of them will fall to the ground apart from the will of your Father. And even the very hairs of your head are all numbered. So don't be afraid; you are worth more than many sparrows. (Matthew 10:29–31)

The Lord will rescue me from every evil

attack and will bring me safely to His heavenly kingdom. To Him to be glory for ever and ever. Amen. **(2 Timothy 4:18)**

[Jesus said,] "I have come that they may have life, and have it to the full." **(John 10:10b)**

[Jesus said,] "And surely I am with you always, to the very end of the age." **(Matthew 28:20b)**

And we know that in all things God works for the good of those who love Him, who have been called according to His purpose. **(Romans 8:28)**

Share what these Bible verses mean to you as you consider a change you have recently experienced, a change you are experiencing now, or a change you anticipate experiencing.

If possible, share another Bible verse(s) you have found meaningful or comforting as you have faced change. Write the Bible references others share.

To Close

Sing or speak the words of the hymn "Abide with Me."

Abide with me, fast falls the eventide.
The darkness deepens; Lord, with me abide.
When other helpers fail and comforts flee,
Help of the helpless, oh, abide with me.

Swift to its close ebbs out life's little day;
Earth's joys grow dim, its glories pass away;
Change and decay in all around I see;
O Thou who changest not, abide with me.

Focusing on the Week Ahead

Sing or speak the words of "Abide with Me" each evening this week. As you do so, reflect upon the "change and decay" you have seen and the comfort you have in knowing that God does not change. He is always with us.

Note changes or proposed changes as reported in the media (television, radio, and print, including your church bulletin or newsletter). In your opinion, which are threats and which are opportunities? Bring to class next week a list of changes that you consider threats and those you consider opportunities.

2

Change—
How Do I Put Up
with the Uncertainties
Caused By Change?

Focusing Our Sights

In this session we will identify the consequences of people's inability to deal with change in their lives, in the lives of others, and in the church. We will explain how God uses change to provide us opportunities to exercise our Christian faith and to spread the Gospel. We will identify life skills we as God's people can adopt and practice to equip ourselves to face the challenges of change. We will cite outcomes that are more likely to occur when we anticipate change with a positive attitude. Finally, we will recognize various ways God equips people to face change through the power of the Holy Spirit working through His Word.

Focusing Our Attention

Share with the group your list of changes reported in the media. Which in your opinion are threats? Why and for whom? Which in your opinion are opportunities? Why and for whom?

Focusing on the Issue

"Things are different than they used to be." Change itself is changing—it's happening with increased speed. How do we put up with the uncertainties caused by proposed and/or actual change? How can we, with the help of God, better deal with change?

Following are some of the typical attitudes we might have as we face change in our lives.

1. Each of us has anticipated change at times as a cynic. As a cynic we see little hope for ourselves or others affected by the change. We stand by the sidelines and watch it "happen," but do not become involved. Cynics wait for change to fail.

2. At times, we have adopted an "eat, drink, and be merry" attitude toward change. This attitude is often accompanied by the statement, "I'm doing fine, don't bother me." There is no hope for the individual, the nation, the world, or the church; so let's make the most of our own merriment while we can and let the rest of the world "go by".

3. We see change coming, we know it must come, but we are unable to cope with what it might bring. We view change with alarm and with resistance. When these stress-filled characteristics become intense, negative physical and emotional consequences may occur.

4. We see change coming; we know it must come. We may serve as a catalyst for the change. We want to know as much about the circumstances, about ourselves, about the results as we can so that we can prepare ourselves and become involved in the change process.

Complete the following inventory. First, check the changes you have experienced. Then rank how well you were able to deal with the change from 1 (good) to 4 (poor).

___ A transfer or move to another city. 1 2 3 4

___ The loss of a job. 1 2 3 4

___ The loss of a loved one
through death. 1 2 3 4

___ An accident that resulted
in serious injury. 1 2 3 4

___ Having children. 1 2 3 4

___ Marital difficulties. 1 2 3 4

___ Demands by one or more
elderly parents. 1 2 3 4

___ Retirement. 1 2 3 4

___ Getting a new boss. 1 2 3 4

___ Getting married. 1 2 3 4

___ Getting divorced. 1 2 3 4

___ Gaining or losing weight. 1 2 3 4

___ Involved in a war. 1 2 3 4

___ Leaving home. 1 2 3 4

___ Going to school as an adult. 1 2 3 4

___ Physical/sexual abuse. 1 2 3 4

___ Other 1 2 3 4

These changes are the result of loss, relocation, and accident or by changes in relationships, personal growth, and health. If you dealt with some changes better than others, what was the reason for the difference?

How did your attitude (positive, negative, Christ-focused, adventuresome, risk-oriented, etc.) at the time of the change or proposed change affect the way you dealt with the change?

Focusing on God's Word

Throughout the ages people have had to deal with change. Perhaps no one dealt with more changes than the apostle Paul. Read **2 Corinthians 11:23–30; 12:9–10.** In these verses Paul recounts some of the experiences he encountered in his life. Underline each of these life-changing experiences. How well would you have coped with the encounters Paul described?

1. What enabled Paul to boast of the things that showed his weakness?

Change often causes us to feel out of control, uncertain, and helpless. St. Paul recognized that as Christ's spokesman of the Gospel he would encounter many life-changing situations. God's love for Paul in Christ motivated and empowered Paul to confess,

> Though I am free and belong to no man, I make myself a slave to everyone, to win as many as possible. To the Jews I became like a Jew, to win the Jews. To those under the law I became like one under the law (though I myself am not under the law), so as to win those under the law. To those not having the law I became like one not having the law (though I am not free from God's law but am under Christ's law), so as to win those not having the law. To the weak I became weak, to win the weak. I have become all things to all men so that by all possible means I might save some. I do all this for the sake of the gospel, that I may share its blessings. (**1 Corinthians 9:19–23**)

2. Circle those words or phrases that indicate Paul's willingness to change and/or face change for the sake of the Gospel.

3. Draw a cross next to the verse that indicates Paul's reason for his willingness to change.

4. Describe what Paul means when he says, "for the sake of the gospel."

Focusing on My Life

"I do all this for the sake of the gospel, that I may share its blessings" **(1 Corinthians 9:23).**

1. What might happen if we were able to face change in our lives with the purpose and resolve of Paul?

2. What keeps you from always having Paul's attitude when you anticipate or experience change?

______ fear

______ loss of safety

______ uncertainty

______ lack of trust

______ skepticism

______ cynicism

______ meism

______ other_________________________

3. Satan will attempt to torpedo any change that might provide us with opportunities to grow in our faith in Jesus and to share the saving faith with others. At times our sinful nature will whisper in our ears, "What's in it for me?" or "I like things the way they are." The world will echo, "Don't rock the boat" and "Don't impose your values on others." Don't feel alone when these thoughts and questions crowd you. Paul continually experienced all of these questions and concerns. Paul confesses, "For what I want to do I do not do, but what I hate I do" (**Romans 7:15**). Paul pleads, "Who will rescue me from this body of death?" (**7:24**).

Paul quickly follows this question with an answer—*the answer*. *The answer* that will forgive you when you fail to see change as a new opportunity to live the new life that is yours through the Gospel. *The answer* that motivated and empowered Paul to face change with confidence. *The answer* that will enable you to overcome fear and doubt when you anticipate change.

The answer:

Therefore, there is now no condemnation for those who are in Christ Jesus, because through Christ Jesus the law of the Spirit of life set me free from the law of sin and death. For what the law was powerless to do in that it was weakened by the sinful nature, God did by sending His own Son in the likeness of sinful man to be a sin offering. (Romans 8:1–3)

Today, tomorrow, the next day, and the

next, God will strengthen our faith as the Holy Spirit works through *the answer* so that when we anticipate or face change we can shout, "Thanks be to God—through Jesus Christ our Lord!" **(Romans 7:25),** who has given me a new opportunity to share His Gospel and who will strengthen and comfort me with His presence as I face yet another change in my life.

4. How can *the answer* change you as you face new things in your life? in your church? in your community?

To Close

Sing or speak the words of this familiar hymn. We ask for His help and guidance as we anticipate and face changes.

Oh, that the Lord would guide my ways
To keep His statutes still!
Oh, that my God would grant me grace
To know and do His will!

Order my footsteps by Your Word
And make my heart sincere;
Let sin have no dominion, Lord,
But keep my conscience clear.

Assist my soul, too apt to stray,
A stricter watch to keep;
If ever I forget Your way,
Restore Your wand'ring sheep.

Make me to walk in Your commands,
A most delightful road;
Nor let my head or heart or hands
Offend against my God.

Focusing on the Week Ahead

1. Memorize one or more of the stanzas of the hymn. Use the hymn as your daily prayer.

2. When our fears of the unknown overtake us, think of the words of **John 3:16** and its promise of eternal life. "For God so loved the world that He gave His one and only begotten Son, that whoever believes in Him shall not perish but have eternal life."

Change— How to Anticipate and Face It

Focusing Our Sights

In this session we will explore how the devil, the world, and our sinful flesh affects our plans and outlook. We will examine the certainties God provides to those who trust in Jesus as their Lord and Savior. Participants will have the opportunity to share their personal philosophies for anticipating, welcoming, dealing with, and using change to accomplish positive results. We will outline a plan for making optimal use of the opportunities for change. Finally, opportunity will be given to express confidence in the hope and power God offers freely in Christ.

Focusing Our Attention

React to the following statements. Do you agree or disagree with them? Why or why not?

"It is in changing that things find purpose." (Heraclitus)

"When we tell ourselves 'I can never change,' or 'That will never happen,' we presume too much and believe too little. In Jesus Christ God renders all of our final conclusions premature and all of our talk of determinism as simply bad faith. In Christ, God opens closed doors, brings resurrection, reveals possibilities, reclaims the lost, liberates the cursed and possessed, and changes the unchangeable." (Don Shelby)

And He [Jesus] said: "I tell you the truth, unless you change and become like little children, you will never enter the kingdom of heaven" **(Matthew 18:3)**.

Focusing on the Issue

We welcome some changes—the changes of seasons, variety in foods, change of scenery in our travels, new job opportunities, improved lifestyle, etc. What change or changes have you or someone you know welcomed recently? Why did you or the person welcome the change?

We resist some changes, particularly those that disrupt our work or life routines, are perceived to lower our prestige, give us less income, are forced on us without an accompanying or satisfying reason, change our relationships with others, reduce our authority, and/or tend to make us feel less than "human". What change or changes have you or someone you know recently resisted? Why did you resist the change?

In contrast, we are usually more eager to accept change if we are involved in the process and are asked to contribute suggestions or opinions, feel that our opinions are respected, understand the reasons and advantages for the change, receive honest feedback, and/or have opportunity to share and pray about change.

Did these factors contribute to your welcoming some changes, while resisting others? If so, how?

Many "formulas" suggest possible ways to deal with change. Add your ideas to the following suggestions.

• Pray for God's guidance.
• Search God's Word for guidance and comfort as you anticipate change.
• Write the facts that you know about the proposed change.
• Write two or more opinions, some of which may express opposing points of view concerning the change.
• Analyze the following aspects of the change: Who will gain from the change? What might be gained? Who will lose from the change? What might be lost because of the change? What is the best time frame for the change (now, in the near future, in the distant future)? Will the projected gain offset the emotional conflict that may result?

Discuss with a partner some change you are currently anticipating or experiencing. Use the suggested steps to analyze the change to determine an appropriate course of action.

Focusing on God's Word

God promises to guide us as we anticipate and face change. What message does each of the following Bible passages speak to you as you consider change.

Moses answered the people, "Do not be afraid. Stand firm and you will see the deliverance the LORD will bring you today. The Egyptians you see today you will never see again. The LORD will fight for you; you need only to be still." (Exodus 14:13–14)

And we know that in all things God works for the good of those who love Him, who have been called according to His purpose. (Romans 8:28)

Be joyful always; pray continually; give thanks in all circumstances, for this is God's will for you in Christ Jesus. (1 Thessalonians 5:16–18)

The God who made the world and everything in it is the Lord of heaven and earth and does not live in temples built by hands. And He is not served by human hands, as if He needed anything, because He Himself gives all men life and breath and everything else. From one man He made every nation of men, that they should inhabit the whole earth; and He determined the times set for them and the exact places where they should live. God did this so that men would seek Him and perhaps reach out for Him and find Him, though He is not far from each one of us. "For in Him we live and move and have our being." As some of your own poets have said, "We are His offspring." **(Acts 17:24–28)**

God is our refuge and strength, an ever-present help in trouble. Therefore we will not fear, though the earth give way and the mountains fall into the heart of the sea, though its waters roar and foam and the mountains quake with their surging. **(Psalm 46:1–3)**

Though the mountains be shaken and the hills be removed, yet My unfailing love for you will not be shaken nor My covenant of peace be removed," says the LORD, who has compassion on you. **(Isaiah 54:10)**

I lift up my eyes to the hills—where does my help come from? My help comes from the LORD, the Maker of heaven and earth. He will not let your foot slip—He who watches over you will not slumber; indeed, He who watches over Israel will neither slumber nor sleep. The LORD watches over you—the LORD is your shade at your right hand; the sun will not harm you by day, nor the moon by night. The LORD will keep you from all harm—He will watch over your life; the LORD will watch over your coming and going, both now and forevermore. **(Psalm 121)**

God guides us and leads us. He knows us and understands us. Through faith in Jesus, God enables us to anticipate and face change with hope and confidence. We have security in Christ Jesus. We are not helpless even though we need help. We are not hopeless for we have hope. God provides us a myriad of guarantees throughout Scripture. God guarantees His help. With pen in hand, review the Bible passages. Underline boldly God's guarantees that speak to you and your needs as you think about change. Explain to a partner how these passages speak to you.

Focusing on My Life

1. Scripture helps us to develop a philosophy and mission for our lives. Talk about a personal philosophy and mission in life that would enable you to welcome, deal with, and use change. After five minutes write your personal philosophy/mission concerning change. Support this with one or more of the Scripture passages studied earlier or other Scripture passages that are particularly meaningful to you.

Now, share your personal philosophy/mission with others in your group.

2. Brainstorm a Christian plan for making optimal use of the opportunities that change provides. Include the group's ideas in the space provided.

To Close

1. Sing or speak the words of the hymn "For All the Saints."

For all the saints who from their labors
    rest,
All who by faith before the world
    confessed,
Your name, O Jesus, be forever blest.
Alleluia! Alleluia!

You were their rock, their fortress,
    and their might;
You, Lord, their captain in the well-
    fought fight;
You, in the darkness drear, their one
    true light.
Alleluia! Alleluia!

Oh, blest communion, fellowship divine,
We feebly struggle, they in glory shine;
Yet all are one within Your great design.
Alleluia! Alleluia!

The golden evening brightens in the
    west;
Soon, soon to faithful warriors comes
    their rest;
Sweet is the calm of paradise the blest.
Alleluia! Alleluia!

2. Develop a group prayer that expresses confidence in the hope and power God offers freely in Christ.

Focusing on the Week Ahead

Reflect upon the words of **Isaiah 44:2:**

"This is what the LORD says—He who made you, who formed you in the womb, and who will help you: Do not be afraid." These promises go with us through the week and through life, to help us face the uncertainties and ambiguities caused by change.

Change— Progress through Change

Focusing Our Sights

In this final session we will focus on the progress the Holy Spirit initiates, working through God's Word. We will define progress as Christ would have us recognize it in our dreams and goals. We will explore examples of positive personal and institutional growth and development in the face of change and plan ways to maximize the potential for a Great Commission life and ministry. We will then celebrate the power our changeless God brings to the life of individual Christians and to His church. Finally, we will thank God for the assurances and certainties that He provides to enable us to plan and dream in eager and joyful anticipation.

Focusing Our Attention

In our journey through life, each of us experiences landmark-type events. Some of them are listed below. Each involves change. Select a partner and discuss what changes are involved and how each occasion provides an opportunity for progress in our lives as Christians.

Birth

Baptism

Confirmation

Graduation

Marriage

Retirement

Death

Can you think of other life experiences that provide progress through change? If so, how?

❖

Focusing on the Issue

1. Write your definition of "progress" as Christ would have us recognize it in our dreams and goals. Discuss your definition with the group. How are definitions similar? different?

2. Think about this progress and how through change you have experienced it in the last year. Take a few moments to list indicator(s) of progress.

3. Think about progress you would like to see in your personal life. What change or changes will be necessary?

4. What specific things will you have to do in order to make this progress?

5. Consider the following.

Progress is made in us through the power of the Holy Spirit working through God's Word. The Gospel has power to produce changes in us. When we acknowledge our sins with true repentance, we receive forgiveness. Our hearts are changed by God's grace.

What specific things might we do as we affirm that "real" progress is made as the Holy Spirit works through God's Word to strengthen faith? How might these things enable us to approach change as a means through which we progress, move forward, to accomplish that which God intends for our lives?

6. Sometimes change is most difficult when it occurs within the church. Why might change within the church be so painful? so necessary?

Check the change(s) you have experienced in your church. Then rank your ability to cope with the change from 1 (good) to 4 (poor). How well did others deal with the change? Put an *X* over the number that best describes others' response to the change.

___ The adoption of a "new" hymnal.   1 2 3 4
___ The arrival of a new pastor.   1 2 3 4
___ The adoption of a new
building program.   1 2 3 4
___ Raises in salary
for all professional staff.   1 2 3 4
___ A change in the role of women
in the church.   1 2 3 4
___ Changes in the worship services.   1 2 3 4
___ Other   1 2 3 4

7. Complete the following sentences:

a. A change I have experienced in my lifetime that has helped the spreading of the Gospel is

b. A change I resisted in my lifetime that has hindered the spreading of the Gospel is

c. As I think about change and the consequences of change, I will ask God to

Focusing on God's Word

Though we change, God does not change. God tells us in **Malachi 3:6–7:** "I the LORD do not change. . . . Return to Me, and I will return to you."

1. God is changeless. We change. The following passages from Scripture use words that mean "change". Discuss with a partner each of the passages. Then describe in your own words what these changes mean to you and how you will use these "power changes" in your response to and relationship with others.

> He saved us, not because of righteous things we had done, but because of His mercy. He saved us through the washing of *rebirth* and *renewal* by the Holy Spirit whom He poured out on us generously through Jesus Christ our Savior, so that, having been justified by His grace, we might become heirs having the hope of eternal life. **(Titus 3:5–7, emphasis added)**

> Therefore, if anyone is in Christ, he is a *new creation*; the old has gone, the new has come! All this is from God, who reconciled us to Himself through Christ and gave us the ministry of reconciliation. **(2 Corinthians 5:17–18, emphasis added)**

> And we, who with unveiled faces all reflect the Lord's glory, are being *transformed* into His likeness with ever-increasing glory, which comes from the Lord, who is the Spirit. **(2 Corinthians 3:18, emphasis added).**

> Do not conform any longer to the pattern of this world, but be *transformed* by the renewing of your mind. Then you will be able to test and approve what God's will is—His good, pleasing, and perfect will. (**Romans 12:2, emphasis added**)

2. Who is the agent for change in each of the passages?

Describe in your own words the change(s) the Holy Spirit has worked in you as you have heard God's Word.

3. What progress has come about through these changes?

4. How do these changes affect you as you experience change in your life? Remember: God's love for you in Jesus never changes. Jesus loved you yesterday and loves you today and will love you tomorrow.

Focusing on My Life

Our changeless God performed a miraculous change in each of us as the Holy Spirit created saving faith within us. Our changeless God continues to perform a miracle in us as the Holy Spirit works through His Word to strengthen and sustain our faith. St. Paul summarizes the change, "And we, who with unveiled faces all reflect the Lord's glory, are being transformed into His likeness with ever-increasing glory, which comes from the Lord, who is the Spirit." **(2 Corinthians 3:18)**

Meditate on God's unchanging love for you. Consider the miraculous transformation God performed in you when He brought you to faith. Contemplate the change God continues to bring about in you as the Holy Spirit working through God's Word strengthens your faith in Jesus.

Now, complete the following sentences.
As I consider change in my life I will first

then I will

and

and

as God in Christ empowers me with His unchanging love.

As I consider change in my church I will first

then I will

and

and

as God in Christ empowers me with His unchanging love.

To Close

1. Read **Psalm 46** in unison.

God is our refuge and strength,
 an ever-present help in trouble.
Therefore we will not fear, though
 the earth give way
and the mountains fall into the heart
 of the sea,
though its water roar and foam
 and the mountains quake with their
 surging.
There is a river whose streams make glad
 the city of God,
 the holy place where the Most High
 dwells.
God is within her, she will not fall;
 God will help her at break of day.
Nations are in uproar, kingdoms fall;
 He lifts His voice, the earth melts.
The LORD Almighty is with us;
 the God of Jacob is our fortress.
Come and see the works of the LORD,
 the desolations He has brought
 on the earth.
He makes wars cease to the ends
 of the earth;
 He breaks the bow and shatters
 the spear,
 He burns the shields with fire.
"Be still, and know that I am God;
 I will be exalted among the nations,
 I will be exalted in the earth."
The LORD Almighty is with us;
 the God of Jacob is our fortress.

2. Pray that as the Holy Spirit works through God's Word, your faith may be strengthened so that you might give thanks and praise to God for change and the new opportunities it will provide for you; opportunities to share your faith in Jesus with unbelievers or with those whose faith is weak.

Focusing on the Week Ahead

Place your hands on your lap or on the table with palms open, facing up. Let them represent your willingness to receive what God has given you. This openness also represents your willingness to share what God has given you—the Good News of salvation in Christ.

Now sing or speak the following stanzas of "Take My Life, O Lord, Renew."

Take my life, O Lord renew,
Consecrate my heart to You;
Take my moments and my days;
Let them sing Your ceaseless praise.

Take my hands and let them do
Works that show my love for You;
Take my feet and lead their way,
Never let them go astray.

Take my voice and let me sing
Praises to my Savior King;
Take my lips and keep them true,
Filled with messages from You.

Take my silver and my gold,
All is Yours a thousandfold;
Take my intellect, and use
Ev'ry pow'r as You shall choose.

Make my will Your holy shrine,
It shall be no longer mine.
Take my heart, it is Your own;
It shall be Your royal throne.

Take my love; my Lord, I pour
At Your feet its treasure store;
Take my self, Lord, let me be
Yours alone eternally.

Notes for the Leader

1—Change—Threat or Opportunity?

❖ Focusing Our Sights

(About 2 minutes.) Read aloud and discuss briefly the goals for this session.

❖ Focusing Our Attention

(About 5 minutes.) **1.** Ask participants to write a definition of change. Allow time for participants to compare their definitions. Write a group definition of change on the chalkboard or a large sheet of newsprint using the definitions composed by individuals.

2. Allow time for participants to work through the questions as they prepare to share an incident of change from their lives. Do not force anyone to share who feels uncomfortable doing so.

❖ Focusing on the Issue

(About 10 minutes.) Read aloud the opening paragraph. Then have volunteers read aloud the three basic levels at which people usually respond to change. Briefly discuss each of the levels. Ask, **At what level do you most often operate when you approach change?** Have participants discuss questions 1–2 with a partner. After a few minutes of discussion, suggest that participants complete the checklist independently. Ask for volunteers to share the items they checked, the items they marked as an

opportunity, and those items they marked as a threat. Ask, **Why is the change reflected in an item an opportunity? a threat?**

Finally, ask participants to identify three "good" changes that have occurred in their lives during the past decade. Allow some time for volunteers to share the changes they identify. Ask, **When you initially anticipated or experienced the change, was it a threat or opportunity? Why was the change good?**

❖ Focusing on God's Word

(About 15 minutes.) Read aloud the opening paragraph. Have participants read **Genesis 3:1–7** silently and then have volunteer read it aloud. Discuss the questions with the whole group, or if your group is large, allow participants to discuss the questions in groups of three.

1. The eyes of Adam and Eve were opened, they realized they were naked, and they made coverings for themselves from fig leaves. The effect of sin is evident in that Adam and Eve realized their nakedness and attempted to cover themselves. For the first time Adam and Eve felt embarrassment, guilt, self consciousness, and shame.

2. Sin destroyed the perfect relationship shared between Adam and Eve, between Adam and God, and between Eve and God. Adam and Eve would experience trouble, heartache, pain, and ultimately death because of their sin.

3. We inherit the sin of Adam and Eve and therefore come into this world separated from God. We experience trouble, heartache, pain, and ultimately death because of our sin and the sins of others.

Read aloud the paragraph that follows the questions. Ask, **What was God's plan?** Without answering the question, ask a volunteer to read aloud **Ephesians 1:4–9.** Ask, **What was God's plan to change us back into what He intended for us?** Allow time for a brief discussion. Urge par-

48

❖

ticipants to complete questions 4–6 with a partner. Discuss their answers with the entire group.

4. Answers will vary. Participants might have underlined any or all of the following words and phrases: *"chose us in Him before the creation of the world to be holy and blameless," "predestined us to be adopted as His sons through Jesus Christ," "redemption through His blood," "forgiveness of sins," "God's grace that He lavished on us with all wisdom and understanding," "made known to us the mystery of His will."*

5. Participants probably will draw a cross next to the phrase *"adopted as His sons through Jesus Christ"* and/or *"In Him we have redemption through His blood."* Emphasize that God brought about the change in us through Jesus' sacrificial act for us. Jesus took the punishment we deserved when He died on the cross. We receive the blessings that Jesus deserved because of His perfect obedience to the Father. Jesus proclaimed victory for us over sin, death, and the power of Satan when He rose from the dead.

6. Answers will vary. God enables us to see change as an opportunity to serve Him and glorify Him. The Holy Spirit works through God's Word to strengthen our faith in Jesus.

❖ Focusing on My Life

(About 15 minutes.) Read aloud the opening paragraph. Have volunteers share a time when they were able to confess, "Yet not as I will, but as You will" (**Matthew 26:39**), as they faced change. Then have volunteers read aloud the Bible passages. Urge participants to underline or circle words and/or phrases that are especially meaningful to them. Allow time for participants to share those words and phrases they marked. Ask, **What do these Bible verses mean to you as you consider a change you have recently experienced, a change you are experiencing, or a change you antici-pate experiencing?** Allow time for participants to share additional Bible verses that have been meaningful or helpful to them as they faced change. Urge participants to write

49

these additional Bible references in the space provided in the Study Guide for future reference.

 To Close

(About 3 minutes.) Sing or speak the stanzas printed from the hymn "Abide with Me." Allow participants to share prayer needs with the entire group or with a partner. Have volunteers pray for the needs identified.

Focusing on the Week Ahead

(About 3 minutes.) Urge participants to complete one or both of the suggested activities prior to the next time the group meets.

2—Change—How Do I Put Up with the Uncertainties Caused by Change?

❖ Focusing Our Sights

(About 2 minutes.) Read aloud and discuss briefly the goals for this session.

❖ Focusing Our Attention

(About 5 minutes.) Ask participants to share with the group the list of changes reported by the media. Ask, **Is this change a threat or an opportunity? Why?** Accept all responses.

❖ Focusing on the Issue

(About 15 minutes.) Read and discuss the opening paragraph. Have participants jot down their answer to the question, "How do we put up with the uncertainties caused by proposed and/or actual change?" Then ask, **How can we with the help of God deal with change better?** Allow time for participants to write their responses to this question in the space provided in the Study Guide. Then ask volunteers to share their answers. Accept all responses. Tell participants that in today's study they will explore answers to that question.

Read aloud and discuss the typical attitudes people usually have toward change. Ask participants to identify their usual attitude. Have participants complete the inventory on

❖

their own. Ask volunteers to share some of their responses. Ask, **Why were you able to deal with some changes better than others?** Discuss the questions that follow the survey with the whole group, or if your group is large, in groups of three or four.

❖ Focusing on God's Word

(About 15 minutes.) Read aloud or have a volunteer read aloud the opening paragraph. Ask participants to number the life-changing experiences that Paul lists in **2 Corinthians 11:23–30; 12:9–10** as you read the verses aloud.

Discuss the question that follows the Bible reference with the entire class. After discussing the question, ask a volunteer to read aloud the paragraph that follows the question.

1. Faith in Jesus Christ enabled Paul to boast of the things that showed his weakness.

Read aloud or ask volunteers to read aloud **1 Corinthians 9:19–23.** Have participants complete the activities that follow with a partner. After most have finished the activities, allow time to share responses with the entire group.

2. Although answers will vary, participants probably circled *"I make," "I became,"* and *"I have become all things to all men so that by all possible means I might save some."*

3. Paul is willing to do all this *"for the sake of the gospel."*

4. Answers will vary. Because of God's great love for Paul demonstrated in the life, death, and resurrection of Jesus, Paul is willing and eager to share God's love with others so that they might share the blessings he has received—forgiveness of sins and eternal life.

❖ Focusing on My Life

(About 15 minutes.) Allow time for participants to discuss the questions either with the entire group or within small groups of three to four participants if the group is large.

52
❖

1–2. Answers will vary.

3. Read aloud or have a volunteer read aloud this section. Emphasize the fact that Satan, the world, and our own sinful self will cause us at times to avoid changes that might give us additional opportunities to share the Gospel. *The answer* is Jesus Christ, who suffered and died to deliver us from death.

4. Jesus Christ and His great love for us comforts us as we face change, and equips and motivates us to recognize change as a new opportunity to share God's love with others.

❖ To Close

(About 5 minutes.) Sing or speak the words to the hymn "Oh, that the Lord Would Guide My Ways."

❖ Focusing on the Week Ahead

(About 3 minutes.) Read aloud the suggested activities. Urge participants to complete one or both of the activities prior to the next time the group meets.

3—Change—How to Anticipate and Face It

❖ Focusing Our Sights

(About 2 minutes.) Read aloud and discuss briefly the goals for this session.

❖ Focusing Our Attention

(About 7 minutes.) Read aloud each of the statements concerning change. Allow time for participants to discuss whether or not they agree or disagree with each.

❖ Focusing on the Issue

(About 15 minutes.) Read aloud the opening paragraph. Then give participants one minute to write responses to the questions. Read aloud the second paragraph. Give participants one minute to write responses to these questions. Read aloud the third paragraph. Once again, give participants one minute to write responses. Allow participants time to discuss their responses with the entire class or within small groups of three to four participants if your class is large.

Ask the entire group, **What formula do you use when dealing with change?** Allow a few volunteers to share and then read aloud the suggested formula. Have participants add their ideas to the list.

Have participants work with a partner to try the suggested formula as they consider a change they are currently anticipating or experiencing. After participants have tried

the formula, ask for evaluations of the formula. **What was helpful? What was not helpful? What additional items might you add to the formula?**

Focusing on God's Word

(About 15 minutes.) Read aloud the opening paragraph. Then read and discuss each of the Bible passages. Ask after each passage is read, **How does this passage speak to you as you anticipate and/or experience change?** Accept all responses.

After reading and discussing all passages, read aloud the closing paragraph of this section. Give participants an opportunity to review independently each of the passages and underline God's guarantees that speak to them and their needs. Allow time for participants to share with a partner how the passages they underlined speak to them personally.

Focusing on My Life

(About 15 minutes.) **1.** Review the Bible passages in Focusing on God's Word. Ask, **How might these passages help you as you develop a personal philosophy/mission concerning change and the way you approach change in your life?** After discussing the question, have individuals write their own personal philosophy and/or mission concerning change. Allow time for volunteers to share their personal philosophy/mission with the entire group.

2. Brainstorm together a Christian plan for making optimal use of the opportunities that change provides to share the love of God in Christ with others. Answers will vary.

To Close

(About 3 minutes.) **1.** Sing or speak the printed words to "For All the Saints."

2. Write a group prayer on the chalkboard or a large sheet of newsprint that expresses confidence in the hope and power God offers freely in Christ. Pray the prayer together.

❖ Focusing on the Week Ahead

(About 2 minutes.) Urge participants to complete the suggested activity prior to the next meeting of the group.

4—Change—Progress through Change

❖ Focusing Our Sights

(About 2 minutes.) Read aloud and discuss briefly the goals for this session.

❖ Focusing Our Attention

(About 10 minutes.) Read aloud the opening paragraph. Have participants work with a partner to discuss how landmark occasions in life provide an opportunity for progress, especially for them as Christians. Allow time for partners to share some of their ideas with the entire group. Ask, **Can you think of other life experiences that provide progress through change?**

❖ Focusing on the Issue

(About 10 minutes.) Have participants complete the questions in this section individually. Then invite them to share their responses to the questions. Answers will vary. Read aloud number 5. Emphasize that progress is made possible through the power of the Holy Spirit working through God's Word. Discuss the questions in depth. Through faith strengthened by the Spirit working through the Gospel, God enables us to affirm change as a means through which God provides us opportunities to serve Him.

Ask, **Why is change sometimes most difficult within**

❖

the church? Why is change necessary within the church?

Have participants complete and then discuss their responses to the change within the church inventory.

Allow time for participants to complete independently the sentence starters that follow the inventory. Ask volunteers to share their responses.

❖ Focusing on God's Word

(*About 15 minutes.*) Read aloud the opening paragraph.

1. Have volunteers read aloud the Bible passages. Emphasize the italicized words that mean change. After each passage is read, allow volunteers to share what the changes referred to in the Bible passages mean to them and how they will use these changes in relationships with others. The changes that God has brought about for and in us enable us to grow in our relationship with Him and with others.

2. God is the agent for change in each of the Bible passages. The Holy Spirit works a renewal of a person's entire life—spirit, will, attitude, and desires.

3–4. Answer will vary.

❖ Focusing on My Life

(*About 10 minutes.*) Read aloud or have a volunteer read aloud the opening paragraphs. Urge participants to complete the sentence starter that focuses on change in their lives and the sentence starter that focuses on change in their church. Provide opportunity for volunteers to share their responses.

❖ To Close

(*About 5 minutes.*) **1.** Read **Psalm 46** in unison.

2. Pray using the suggestions in the Study Guide.

 # Focusing on the Week Ahead

(About 2 minutes.) Urge participants to complete the sug-gested activity during the next week.

Real lives facing real frustrations need Connections to God and to one another.

The **Connections** Bible study series helps take the concerns of your heart and turn them over to Jesus in worship, prayer, Bible study and discussion.

Connections uses a Gospel-centered message to build trust in God and to develop trusting and supportive relationships with one another, just as Christ intended.

Connections studies look at small portions of Scripture that really hit home, in areas where anxiety is often deepest.

For small groups or individual study, **Connections** uses God's Word to build relationships and bring peace to troubled hearts.

Ask for **Connections** at your Christian bookstore.

H54742

3558 SOUTH JEFFERSON AVENUE
SAINT LOUIS MISSOURI 63118-3968